MW01618585

Evan,
Always Believe You
CAN!
Miriam
Laundes
2014

I CAN

BELIEVE IN MYSELF

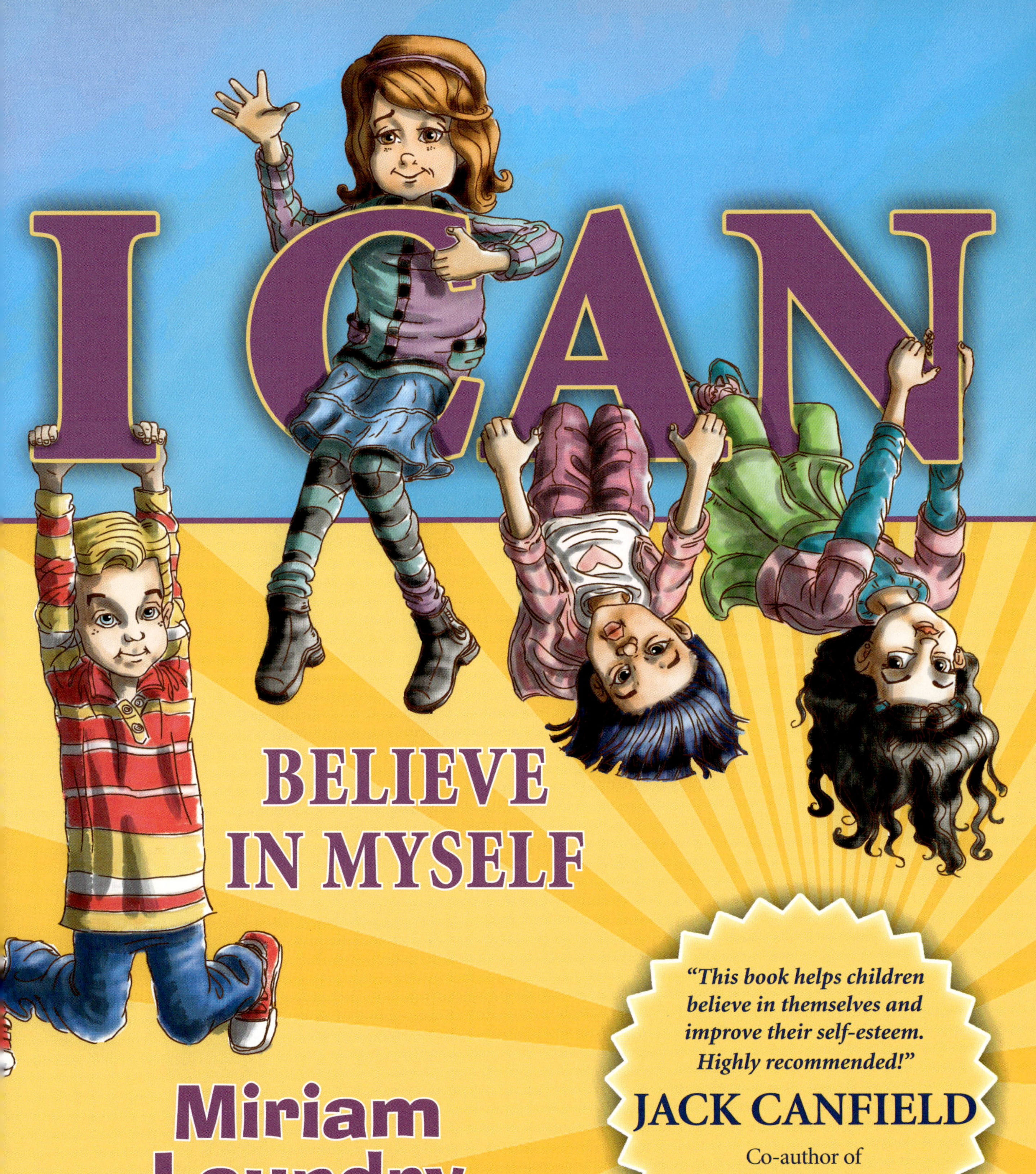

Miriam Laundry

pictures by Jenniffer Julich

Photography by Terri Schous Photography

Cover Design by Jenniffer Julich

Layout by Electra Communications

Editing by Brian Cretney

www.LaundryBooks.com

ISBN 978-0-9918694-1-1 Paperback

ISBN 978-0-9918694-0-4 Hardback

Printed in Canada

Cataloguing in Publication Data available upon request from Library and Archives Canada.

FIRST EDITION

In memory of our beloved Freya.
You are the reason I started writing.

"Please don't say Molly, please don't say Molly," Molly silently begged.

"Our next Star of the Day is …

MOLLY!" said Mrs. Ruby as she picked a card.

"Please bring a Show-and-Tell to share with the class tomorrow."

After school, Molly walked home with only one thing on her mind.

"I CAN'T speak in front of the class.

I just CAN'T," she thought.

Molly felt sick
to her stomach.

She thought about it at dinner…

…during her bath...

…until she fell asleep.

The next day, Molly went to school early to talk with Mrs. Ruby.

"**I CAN'T** be the Star of the Day today," she blurted, "because a three-headed monster took my Show-and-Tell!"

"A three-headed monster?" responded Mrs. Ruby with a smile. "I wonder what the monster needed your Show-and-Tell for?"

"Probably to use for *his* Show-and-Tell," Molly said.

"Well, okay. You can be the Star of the Day *tomorrow*," said Mrs. Ruby as she continued to shred paper.

Molly stood quietly for a moment.

"What is that?" she asked, curiously watching the machine.

"This is called a paper shredder. It cuts up paper and gets rid of it," explained Mrs. Ruby.

"Wow, it looks hungry!" said Molly as the bell rang.

As the children made their way into the classroom, Maria handed a note to Mrs. Ruby.

It read: *"I will be picking Maria up early today for an appointment."*

That gave Molly an idea.

The next day, Molly walked straight to the teacher's desk and put a piece of paper in front of her.

"You poor thing," sighed Mrs. Ruby, "you will have a difficult time talking with your friends today."

Molly bit her nails. She hadn't thought of that!

Molly sat on a swing
at recess watching
her friends play.
"Hey,
Molly..."

"Molly, can you push me, please?" asked Maria.

"I CAN'T swing by myself,

I just CAN'T."

Molly wanted to tell her to try but she saw Mrs. Ruby and remembered the note.

She knew Maria could do it if she just tried…but Molly couldn't talk. So she gave Maria a push.

"Come on!
It's your turn."

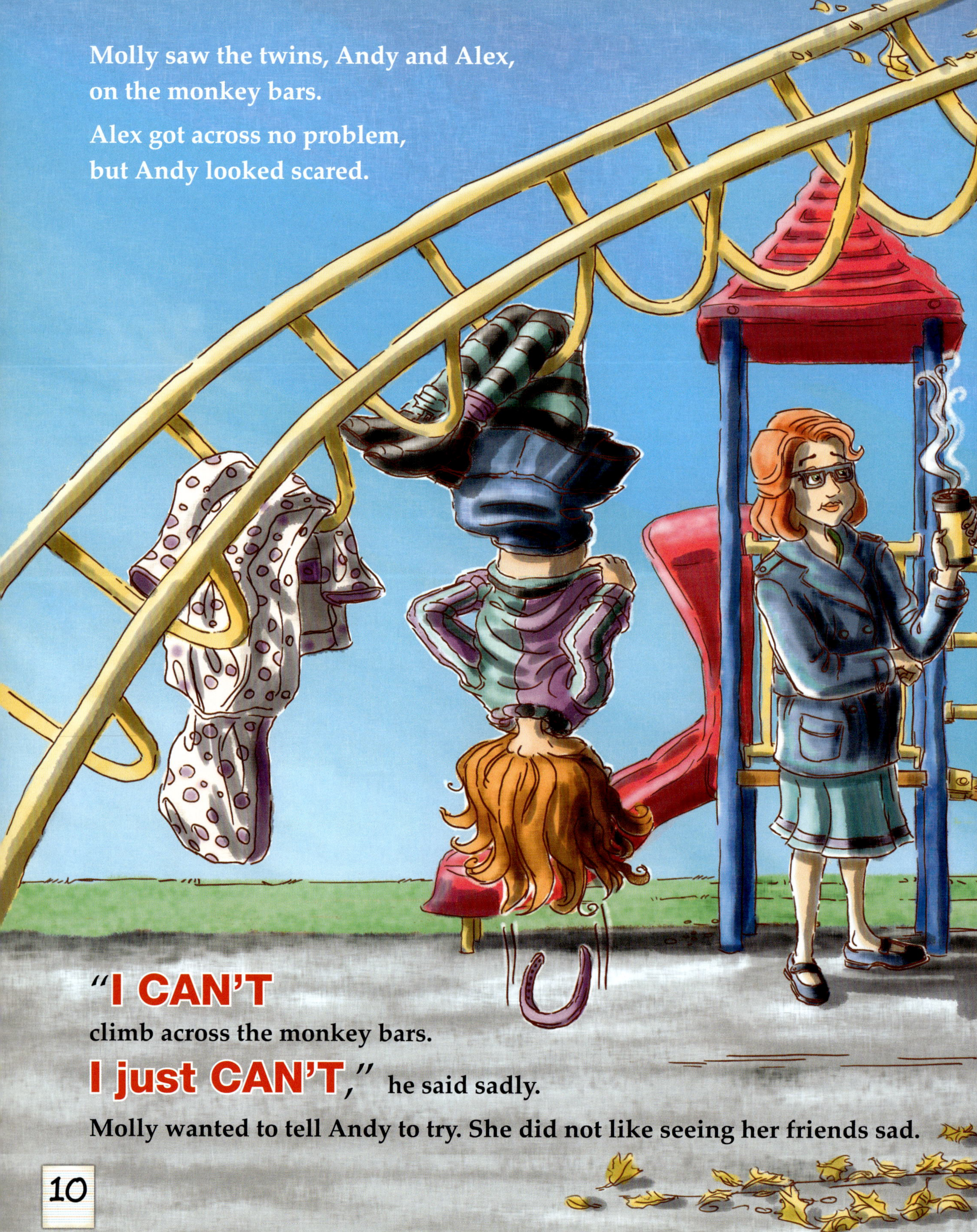

Molly saw the twins, Andy and Alex, on the monkey bars.

Alex got across no problem, but Andy looked scared.

"I CAN'T

climb across the monkey bars.

I just CAN'T," he said sadly.

Molly wanted to tell Andy to try. She did not like seeing her friends sad.

She was sure he could do it
if he just tried…but
she couldn't talk.
"Ouch!"

Molly heard Emily.

She had tripped over her shoelaces playing tag.

"**I CAN'T** tie my shoelaces, **I JUST CAN'T**," said Emily wiping away tears. "Can you tie them for me?"

Molly knew Emily could do it if she just tried…
but Molly couldn't talk.

So she tied Emily's shoelaces for her.

Molly ran to the field.

"Why does everyone keep saying **I CAN'T***?"* she wondered.

She thought about it a lot – even during craft time.

Suddenly, Molly realized something. *She* had been using those same words *herself*.

Late that night, Molly rummaged through her craft materials.

"This is my best idea yet!" she said with a smile as bright as the moon.

The next morning, Molly hurried to school.

"Mrs. Ruby," Molly said out of breath, "I need your help to get my Show-and-Tell ready."

"What do you need?" asked Mrs. Ruby.

Molly looked in the hallway to make sure no one could hear.

"Top Secret," Molly said. Then she whispered in Mrs. Ruby's ear.

"Let me pour myself another coffee," said Mrs. Ruby with a curious grin.

"**I CAN'T** make it through the morning without my coffee.

I JUST CAN'T."

Molly cut, coloured and pasted.

Just as Molly added her final touches, the bell rang.

When the children had settled into their seats, Mrs. Ruby announced,

"Class, our Star of the Day is...**MOLLY**!"

Molly stood up, took a deep breath and walked to the front of the class.

"My mom always tells me to make good choices," started Molly.

"Yesterday, I finally understood why. I kept telling myself

'**I CAN'T**' speak in front of the class, so I wasn't even trying!"

Molly wrote on a piece of paper as Mrs. Ruby uncovered the Show-and-Tell.

Molly had decorated the paper shredder.

"This is my friend, Shreddy. He is really hungry and I am going to feed him this piece of paper. Anything Shreddy eats is gone forever."

She handed her paper to Mrs. Ruby.

"Good bye, **'I CAN'T'** SPEAK IN FRONT OF THE CLASS," announced Molly.

Shreddy swallowed the paper so fast.

said Molly in a deep voice pretending to be Shreddy.

"**I CAN** speak in front of the class because...
I BELIEVE I CAN!" said Molly proudly.

"I want to try!" said Maria walking up to Shreddy.

She wrote on a piece of paper and said, "Good bye, **'I CAN'T'** SWING BY MYSELF."

Shreddy swallowed the paper so fast.

declared Molly and Maria.

"I CAN!" said Maria proudly.

"Does anyone else want to feed Shreddy?" asked Molly.

Andy went up.

"Good bye, **'I CAN'T'** CLIMB ACROSS THE MONKEY BARS."

Shreddy swallowed the paper so fast.

said Andy, Molly and Maria.

"I CAN!" shouted Andy.

One by one, all the children went up.

Last was Emily.

"Good bye, **'I CAN'T'** TIE MY SHOELACES."

Shreddy swallowed the paper so fast.

the whole class joined in.

"I CAN!" said Emily smiling.

"Is there anyone else?" asked Molly.

Everyone looked at each other but it was Emily who spoke.

"Everyone has already gone. There is no one left."

"There is still *one* person," spoke up Mrs. Ruby.

She took a piece of paper and wrote on it:

"YUM YUM YUM," cheered the whole class.

More Praises...

"Miriam Laundry's debut children's book is a wonderful story that helps kids discover the power of believing in themselves. Beautifully expressive illustrations highlight some of the important challenges that young kids face and bring the book to life. I'm already looking forward to the next book in the series. I highly recommend this book!"

Sheri Fink

#1 International Best-selling, Award-Winning Children's Author of *The Little Rose, The Little Gnome* and *The Little Firefly*

"I CAN" is a charming picture book that addresses a real childhood fear for many: public speaking. But its message is much broader than that. This heart-warming and humorous story will connect with all children who have convinced themselves that any goal is beyond their reach. And the playful illustrations will keep the young reader smiling all the way through. This is a book that will be requested time and time again. A must-have for every parent and teacher."

Brian Cretney

Elementary School Teacher and Award-Winning Author of *Tooter's Stinky Wish* and *Last in Line*

"This lovely story roused so many of my own 'I CAN'T' specters from childhood. How I wish I'd had access to such a simple and happy means of empowerment back then. Thanks, Miriam Laundry, for making life a little easier for young people through this inspiring book."

Barry A. Benson

Executive Director, 826CHI.org and Author of *The Bubble Gum Machine*

"I CAN" Book Series

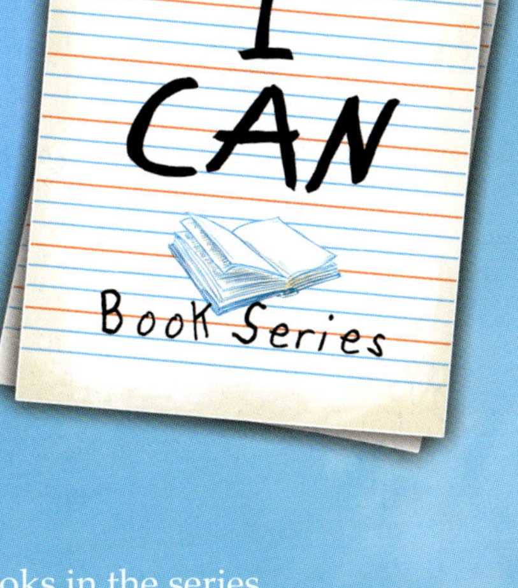

The "I CAN" book series empowers children to believe in themselves and their abilities.

It is this "I CAN" attitude that helps raise confident individuals. Once children understand they are responsible for their results, they are able to make changes.

The words that follow I CAN become very important. This is the reason we bring you the "I CAN" book series.

"I CAN…Believe in Myself"
"I CAN…Make a Difference"(Look for it in 2014!)

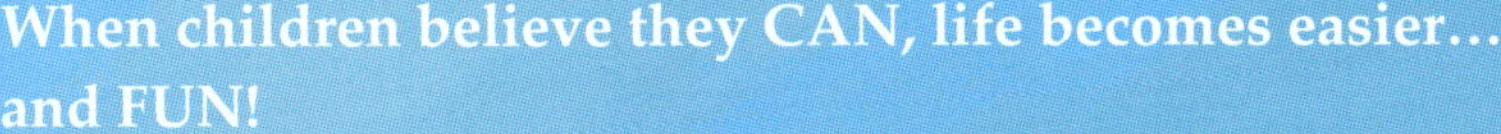

When children believe they CAN, life becomes easier… and FUN!

Become a Fan and keep up to date on the release of upcoming books in the series.

www.Facebook.com/MiriamLaundryFanPage
www.LaundryBooks.com

COMING 2014 – "I CAN…Make a Difference"

About the Illustrator

Jenniffer Julich is often on the hunt for the perfect visual that not only describes the text, but also enhances it to emotionally pull the reader into the mind's eye of the author.

Jenniffer Julich is the primary illustrator at Jnnffr Productions.

www.jnnffr.com

This book belongs to:

and **I CAN...**

I CAN SPEAK in front of the Class

I CAN CLIMB across the monkey bars

I CAN SWING by myself

I CAN tie my shoe laces